The HAIR Book

The HAIR Book

For Jebb Gardiner Tether,
with love

The HAIR Book

by Graham Tether · illustrated by Roy McKie

A Bright & Early Book

From BEGINNER BOOKS   A Division of Random House, Inc., New York

HAIR!
HAIR!
It's everywhere!

Some have a little.

Some have lots.

Plain hair

Striped hair

Polka dots.

Curls

and braids

and beards and lashes.

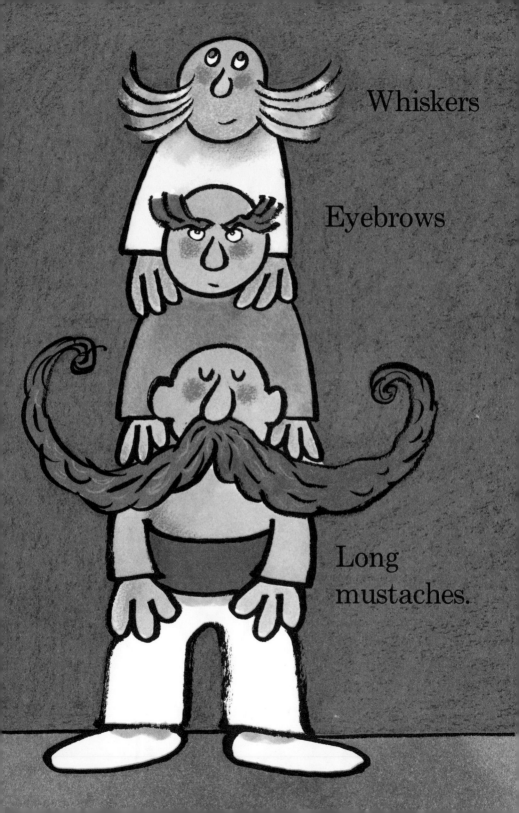

Whiskers

Eyebrows

Long
mustaches.

Dark hair

Fair hair

Wig hair

Bear hair.

Everybody seems to wear hair.

So many different
kinds of hair!

Lambs have woolly
coats to wear.

Pigs have bristles.
They don't care.

And porcupines
have quills that scare.

With hair there's
so, so much to do...

Wash it

Dry it

Braid it

Dye it . . .

Curl it

Clip it

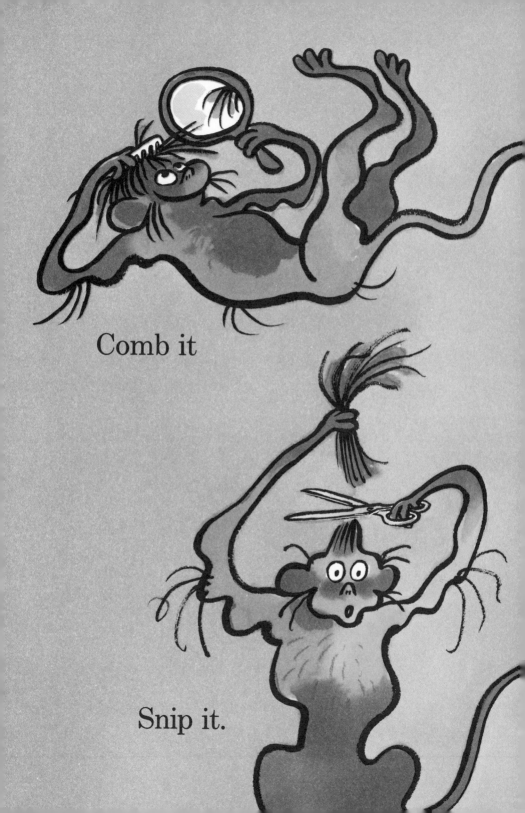

Comb it

Snip it.

And think of the things
that you could do
if your hair just grew ...

and GREW ...

and GREW!

You could make
a ladder
with your hair . . .

or be the maypole
at the fair.

And if you grew
a long goatee . . .

you could use your hair
to water-ski!

Fish

and snails—

do they have hair?

Not one hair.
Not anywhere.

Be glad you're not
a fish or snail.

Be glad you're not
a hairless whale ...

a frog,

a turtle,

or a snake.

Enjoy your hair,
for goodness' sake!

Plain

or dyed,

loose

or tied . . .

curly

or straight...

HAIR IS GREAT!